Mrs. Wells.

C000081356

A TALE OF THREE PIE

A peep into the past of the Blackpool piers

by

JON DE JONGE

A Tale of Three Piers: A peep into the past of the Blackpool piers
by Jon de Jonge
Published by Lancashire County Books, 143 Corporation Street, Preston
Copyright ©Jon de Jonge, 1993
Typeset by Carnegie Publishing Ltd., 18 Maynard Street, Preston
Printed by T. Snape & Co., Preston

ISBN 1-871236-28-2

All rights reserved
No part of this publication may be reproduced, stored in a retrieval system, or transmitted in any form or by any means
mechanical, electronic, photocopying, recording or otherwise, without the prior permission of the publishers.

Contents

Foreword

IN 1993 THE SOUTH PIER is 100 years old, the Central Pier 125 and the North Pier 130 years old, so it seems that this is an appropriate time to have a brief look at their very varied history. In a small booklet one can only glance superficially at the many topics and I apologise for the inevitable omissions. As always, the hardest task is to decide what to leave out (for example, the proposed Claremont and Palatine Piers). Virtually every subject—the steamers, entertainment, refreshments, amusements, the shops, and so on—all of them deserve a book of their own.

I hope this souvenir publication will appeal to both residents and visitors, reminding us just how rich is Blackpool's heritage, and showing us also how promising the future is for the piers.

Many people have helped and encouraged me in this work, and I would like to express my heart-felt gratitude to all of them, but in particular to Ted Lightbown of the Blackpool and Fylde Historical Society, the staff of the Blackpool Central Library, Bob Eastleigh and David Bateman of the National Piers Society, Esme Darrick, Mr A. P. Maitland, Brian Crompton of First Leisure, Peter Walters of the North Pier, David Pearce of the *Evening Gazette*, the Lancashire Record Office, North West Film Archive, George Hill of the Blackpool Tourist Office, and Richard Baguley of Cartmell PR. I am particularly indebted to Cyril Critchlow (currently working on a comprehensive survey of Blackpool showbusiness) and Jack Greenwood, who have both generously given me the benefit of their researches, and to Matthew Kelly and Russ Abbot for their enthusiastic support.

'Last but not least' may sound like a cliché, but anyone who has tried to write will know how true it is. I am eternally indebted to Lyn, my wife, for her artwork, co-writing, proof-reading, her battles with a strong-willed word processor, and, finally, her typing and tolerance.

1. *Walk over the sea*

MOST VISITORS CAME TO BLACKPOOL by farm wagon, stage coach, horseback or on foot in the early nineteenth century. In addition there were a few brave, well-to-do passengers from the ships en route from Liverpool and Fleetwood, who were ferried ashore in fishing boats.

With the opening of the railway line in 1846 Blackpool developed rapidly and during the 1850s there was a growing demand for the town to have its own pier.

The expansion and improvement of the town was, therefore, already under way when, in 1861, a group of the town's citizens met in the Clifton Arms Hotel to discuss building a pier. Their aim was not just to attract more steamboat trade but also to cater for the fashionable Victorian exercise—strolling in the open air. A pier would provide 'greater promenading space . . . a safe means for visitors to walk over the sea'.

Figure 1: Inauguration poster, 1862.

At a Meeting held in Blackpool,
on the 31st day of December, 1861,
the following Gentlemen were appointed a Provisional Committee to form a Company to erect a

PIER AT BLACKPOOL:—

CHARLES HENRY WAINWRIGHT, BLACKPOOL.
CHARLES JOHN GALLOWAY, MANCHESTER.
HENRY THOMAS WILSON, BLACKPOOL
WILLIAM CATTERALL,
JOHN ECCLESTON,
WILLIAM BIRCH,
JOSEPH SMITH,
JOHN WADE,
CHARLES EDWARD CHADWICK,
RICHARD COOKSON, WARTON.
WILLIAM PORTER, FLEETWOOD.
ADOLPHUS SIGFRIED VIENER, BLACKPOOL.
EDWARD BLANE.

On February 10th, 1862, K. Birch, of London, was elected Civil Engineer to the Company.

The Contract for Erection was given to LAIDLOW and Sons, of Glasgow, on March 12, 1862.

THE FIRST PILE OF THE

NOBLE AND MAGNIFICENT PIER,
INAUGURATED THIS DAY,
Was driven by Captain Preston, Chairman of the Directors, on April 27th, 1862.

DIRECTORS.

MR. A. M. VIENER,   MR. F. ANYON,
„ R. RAWCLIFFE,   „ T. H. LEWIS,
„ W. BIRCH,   „ H. C. Mc CREA.
„ M. SATTERTHWAITE,

Length of Pier, 1358 feet; Width do., 28 feet; Supposed weight of metal, 12,000 Tons.

CAPTAIN PRESTON, Chairman.   E. BLANE Secretary.

Printed during the Inaugural Procession, by J. Waddington, Church Street, Blackpool.

Figure 2: The North Pier, from the Illustrated London News, *1863*
Many pier opening festivities in other resorts were covered by this famous journal, which gave full reports as well as excellent drawings.

2. Opening ceremony

IT WAS A GRAND DAY FOR BLACKPOOL when its first pier (the North) was opened on Thursday 21 May 1863 with great pomp and circumstance and bands playing 'The Blackpool Pier Polka'. Houses and streets were decorated with flags, as was the pier itself, and crowds flocked into the town for the event.

Major Preston, the chairman of the pier directors, must have been a visionary when he declared in his opening speech that with the pier 'Blackpool would take a progressive step and out-rival other towns'.

The pier was a great success from the very beginning. In the first year there were 275,000 admissions, 400,000 in 1864 and 465,000 in 1865. The income in 1866 was £2,800 and expenditure £800. It was a lucrative investment, rarely paying below 12 per cent dividend.

Figure 3: Order of opening procession, 1863.

OPENING PROCESSION

The Volunteer Artillery,
Deputations of Freemasons, Oddfellows,
Board of Health,
Manchester City Band,
The Trades of Blackpool:—
the Butchers, the Joiners, the Painters,
the Printers,
the Boatmen with a mounted boat,
the Blacksmiths, the Stonemasons,
the Shrimpers,
the Fire Engine,
Juvenile Brass Band of the Manchester
Ragged and Industrial Schools,
Ancient Order of Druids (with two
High Priests in full costume, and a
Bard mounted on an ass),
Independent Order of Mechanics,
The Bathing Vans, the Hackney Carriages,
the Donkeys and the Chimney Sweep.

Figure 4 (right): The South (Central) Pier, 1870.
From Blackpool's Progress *(1926, now reprinted by*
Blackpool and Fylde Historical Society).
A very simple structure at first, the South Pier gradually
became festooned with advertisements, causing many
complaints from residents and the town council.

Figure 5 (left): The Bickerstaffe, 1879.
The most modern ship of her day, she was in service
for nearly fifty years. Already playing a major
part in Blackpool's progress, the Bickerstaffe
family were to take on the biggest role of
all—promoting, against strong opposition, the
Blackpool Tower.

3. *Arrival of a rival*

THE NORTH PIER WAS SO SUCCESSFUL that within three months of its opening Major Preston suggested building another pier, further south, to accommodate the 'excursionist class'. Opposition from the North Pier was so bitter that Major Preston resigned from the board of directors and his name was erased from the foundation stone.

Nevertheless the plans went ahead and the Blackpool South Jetty Company Limited was formed in 1864. Work began in July 1867 and the pier, called at first the South Pier or South Jetty, opened on 30 May 1868. (The name was changed to the Central Pier in 1893, when Blackpool's third pier, the Victoria, was opened.)

However, according to the *Preston Pilot* of May 1868, quoted by Kathleen Eyre, 'the novelty of the piers was waning . . . the proceedings passed off tamely, there not being any attempt at a public ceremony'.

The business was equally quiet, almost disastrous, until 'Young Bob' Bickerstaffe took over in 1870. Counting thirteen people on the pier, compared with a crowded North Pier, he decided that something had to be done. He organised a cheap steamer excursion to Southport, charging 1s. instead of 2s., had handbills printed and took them round the town himself. Two hundred and fifty passengers turned up and while they were on board Bob searched for a band.

When the trippers returned, a German band was playing for them and they started dancing on the pier deck, most of them staying all evening.

The steamer excursions and dancing changed the fortunes of the pier and it was to be famous for dancing in the open air for the next hundred years. Young Bob's appeal to the masses earned it the title of the 'People's Pier'.

Diversified Day Excursions

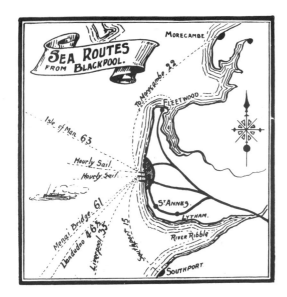

Figure 6: Guide to Steamboat Sailings, *1912.*
(Courtesy of the Central Library, Blackpool.)

North Pier Steamship Company
⊕✦⊕
Grand Sea Excursions.

Also Hourly Sails from the Pier.

Figure 7: The Greyhound *interior,*
from Breezy Blackpool, *1899. (Courtesy of C. Critchlow.)*

4. Full steam ahead!

THE STEAMBOAT TRADE caused intense rivalry between the North and Central Piers but the Central had the advantage because 'Young Bob' Bickerstaffe was the coxswain of the lifeboat and knew the coastline so well. Also the Central ran Sunday trips, whereas the North Pier did so only briefly. (Some members of the North Pier Board objected to this loss of trade!)

The ships tried to outdo each other—the trip to Douglas, for instance, over sixty miles, was reduced to under three hours' sailing time. In 1895 both piers set up individual steamer companies, buying large paddle steamers for the Isle of Man service. The Central had the *Queen of the North* and the North Pier had the *Greyhound*. In 1904 the North bought the *Deerhound* but the company was unprofitable and it was sold.

During the Great War of 1914–18 the danger from U-boats restricted pleasure trips to a limit of three miles. This meant that the ships plying from the piers could only go as far as Southport. In 1916 the *Greyhound* was requisitioned and soon after so was the *Queen of the North*. On 20 July 1917 the *Queen of the North* was sunk with all hands whilst mine-sweeping in the North Sea.

After the war sailings were resumed but trade was never very good because of other competing amusements. It was abandoned in 1939.

Figure 8: Captain Harry of the Queen of the North. *From* Guide to Steamboat Sailings, *1908.*

Blackpool Passenger Steamboat Company, Limited.

VISIT THE CENTRAL PIER.

HEALTH AND PLEASURE.

Two Quadrille Bands

Daily.

LARGEST DANCING PLATFORM
IN ENGLAND.

Sacred Music on Sundays,

AFTERNOON AND EVENING,
BY THE COMBINED PIER BANDS.

ADMISSION to the Pier, 2d.
Four Day Tickets, 8d. | Seven Day Tickets, 1s.

CENTRAL PIER.

Grand
Sea Excursions Daily

BY THE NEW MAGNIFICENT CROSS-CHANNEL
SALOON PASSENGER STEAMER

" Queen of the North,"
" Bickerstaffe,"
" Wellington,"
And other
First-class
Steamers,

To Douglas, Isle of Man ; Llandudno ; Bangor ;
Barrow, for Furness Abbey and the Lake District ;
Menai Straits ; Liverpool ; Morecambe.

Hourly and other Short Sea Excursions.

Figure 9: Advertisement from Breezy Blackpool, *2nd edn., 1901. (Courtesy of Mr A. P. Maitland.)*

We are sailing—again!

AFTER A GAP of more than half a century the North Pier decided to reintroduce some sea excursions in 1992. Unfortunately the plans were beset by many problems. Bad weather prevented the paddle steamer *Waverley* from visiting in May 1992. She was held up in the Clyde estuary by severe storms.

The *Balmoral*, a diesel-powered 1949 ship, paid three visits in September but the third had to be cancelled because of rough seas. The captain tried for half an hour to dock at the jetty, but in vain. The *Balmoral* was forced to turn back to Llandudno leaving well over a hundred disappointed would-be passengers staring incredulously out to sea.

Figure 10: The Balmoral *at North Pier jetty, September 1992. (Photo by Jon de Jonge.)*

What the papers said . . .

THE SOUTH PIER

'The People's Pier'—as Mr Bickerstaffe delights to call the structure over which he rules supreme—is quite ready to receive the crowds of visitors which are expected to arrive in Blackpool during the weekend. Dancing will, as usual, form the staple of the attractions of this pier, and the directors have done wisely to engage a band at a fixed salary—thus doing away with that continual appearance of the collection box which formed a source of inconvenience to dancers in previous seasons. The 'Wellington', the 'Great Western' and other steamers will ply for hourly and other trips.

Gazette & News, 11 June 1886

`THE PIER OF THE DEMOCRACY´

Mr R. Bickerstaffe has indeed captured the favour of the masses, as a visit to the pier on any summer day will undeniably show. Dancing will again be the principal attraction for Whitsuntide. This exercise is one of the most popular means Lancashire workpeople have of obtaining the necessary relaxation from the cares and worries of everyday life, and in view of the large crowds which are expected this week two bands have been engaged.

Gazette & News, 3 June 1892

If you wish to Spend the Day with Pleasure, Visit the
CENTRAL PIER
BLACKPOOL,
Where you can have Genial and Pleasant Exercise, coupled with a Bracing Sea Breeze.
TWO QUADRILLE BANDS
On two of the finest OPEN-AIR DANCING PLATFORMS in England. Hours of attendance during Whit-Week: From 9-0 a.m. until 12-30 p.m.; from 2-0 until 5-0 p.m.; and from 7-0 until 10-0 p.m.
Note the Great Novelty—
DANCING OVER THE SEA
A First-Class Fleet of STEAMERS ply from the Pier Head for long and short Sea Excursions. See Bills at Pier Entrance.
Admission to the Pier, 2d. Four-days Tickets, 6d. Weekly Tickets, 10d. All other Tickets equally cheap.
R. BICKERSTAFFE, Manager.

Figure 11: Gazette and News, *4 June 1895.*

Pier Head,
MORNING, AFTERNOON, AND EVENING.

Open-Air

Dancing

ON AN

Entirely New Pitch-Pine Floor.

MILITARY BAND.

Figure 12: Guide to Steamboat Sailings, *1910.*

5. *Dance over the sea*

With grim-set faces, with a Wellington-at-Waterloo expression, the Lancashire Lad and Lass take their dancing seriously. Wearing thick boots their tread is something short of a pile-driver and the stoutest-hearted flooring quakes and trembles beneath the percussion.

Globe magazine, quoted in *Blackpool Story*

PLAYING POLKAS, quadrilles, barn dances and the Lancers, the 'German bands' or Quadrille bands on the Central Pier played three sessions a day, sometimes starting very early for the day-trippers—5.30 a.m! In 1873 the band was paid £3 10s. between them for a six-day week (Sundays extra), and they supplemented their earnings by passing a collection round amongst the dancers. By 1886 a nine-piece band was hired at a full, fixed rate of £12 7s. 6d. and the collection box disappeared.

The popularity of dancing did have its drawbacks. On one occasion a party of Welsh miners went on the rampage because the band did not have the sheet music for their request.

Residents complained of dancing lowering the tone of the area and in 1891 strongly objected to plans for the shore-end White Pavilion to be used for dancing. The North Pier did not allow dancing—even 'comic singing' was frowned upon. The piers catered for opposite markets and the director of the North Pier Board, Mr H. McCrea, summed it up, 'I think it is a good idea that the working classes can enjoy themselves without the surveillance of the other classes.'

Despite competition from the Raikes Hall Gardens, the Belle Vue Strawberry Gardens and Uncle Tom's Cabin, the Central Pier still maintained its popularity for open-air dancing and continued long after the others had declined.

During the 1930s there was a wide variety of entertainments on the piers and the holiday guidebooks of the time specifically mention the open-air dancing on the Central Pier:

Figure 13: Dancing on Central Pier, from a postcard dated 1903. (Courtesy of Mr P. Jackson.)

The Central Pier possesses the novel attraction of open-air dancing, while artistes of national fame appear in the Pavilion, and one can spend a very enjoyable time on this pier.

Holiday Journal, 1934.

The three piers have six roomy pavilions in which first-rate entertainment, both classical and popular, is dispensed . . . On the Central Pier is open-air dancing and games, and a very enjoyable concert party performs at the pier head.

Holiday Journal, 1935.

North Pier.—Promenade Concerts by the NORTH PIER ORCHESTRA. The SPARKLETS CONCERT PARTY. " ON WITH THE SHOW," a New Style Entertainment. THE ROUMANIAN BAND.

Central Pier.—" A JOLLY GOOD COMPANEE," with MURIEL GEORGE and ERNEST BUTCHER, of Broadcast Fame. Dancing in the Open Air.

Victoria Pier.—VICTORIA PIER ORCHESTRA in the Floral Hall. ERNEST BINNS' " ARCADIAN FOLLIES." The VICTORIA PLAYERS in the Pavilion.

Figure 14: Autumn guide, 1930.

In his book *Blackpool Entertains the Troops* Jack Greenwood, as well as talking about the war-time shows, gives an excellent description of the dancing on the Central Pier in the 1940s

. . . the strains of dance music would be heard coming from the end of Central Pier . . . Tony Lewis and his Swingsters from dawn till dusk would be swinging away so that holidaymakers and locals too could trip around a new dance floor on the pier's planks. What a mecca this not too large area of polished planking became, sheltered from the wind on three sides, virtually non-stop dancing to a band which would fluctuate in numbers from perhaps half a dozen to the size of a full Paul Whiteman type concert orchestra . . . Weather permitting the Central Pier dance band packed them in, the main problem for those wanting to dance was simply to get in the dance area. Dancers had to fight their way down the pier and having got there fight their way onto the floor. Exercise enough in itself but they loved it. Romantic too under a sky of blue holding on to someone you've probably never met before gliding across the floor to the tender 'Boomps a Daisy'. Boys and girls 'clicked' as never before, or since. The music breathed romance as male arms encircled slim unknown waists.

After the Second World War, however, open-air dancing became less popular. Most of the centre platform became the open-air theatre in 1949 and the pier-head dance floor became the New Theatre in 1967. Dancing was moved indoors to the shore-end White Pavilion. Built in 1903, this was used for pierrot shows, revues, and Peter Webster's shows until 1966, when it was demolished to make way for the Dixieland Palace and Golden Goose Complex.

Costing £150,000, the Palace opened in 1967 and had 'the biggest bar service in Britain' (*Evening Gazette*, 29 May 1968). Music for dancing was provided by jazz groups, show bands (Eric Delaney, for instance), pop groups and discos. Now the Oz Disco, the Palace also has a full winter schedule.

Figure 15: The White Pavilion, Central Pier, in the 1930s.
(Photograph courtesy of Ted Lightbown.)

6. *Sounds of sweet music*

GRAND OPEN-AIR

PROMENADE CONCERTS

Daily
10-0 to 1-0,
2-30 to 4-30,
7-30 to 10-0
(except
Saturday
evening.)

Over the Sea, by

Mr. G. E. JOHNSON'S

ORCHESTRE-DE-SALON.

Admission to the Pier and Concerts 2d.

IN THE PAVILION

EVENING CONCERT

ON SATURDAY, 6TH JUNE, AT 7-45.

VOCALIST—

Miss EDITH LONSDALE.

SOLO VIOLIN	MR. J. HULME.
SOLO FLUTE	MR. MARSDEN.
SOLO CORNET	MR. REYNOLDS.

ORCHESTRE-DE-SALON,

CONDUCTOR MR. G. E. JOHNSON.

Admission 2d. (Including Pier). Front Seats 6d.
(Including Pier).

Figure 16: Gazette & News, *June 1891.*

The 'other classes' had refined entertainments provided for them on the North Pier by an orchestra of thirty-five players in the Indian Pavilion. As Simon Adamson says in *Seaside Piers*, the North Pier concerts 'became famous throughout the country . . . orchestral music of the highest order followed upon the appointment of Edward de Jong' as conductor. A principal flautist with the Hallé for thirteen years, he later ran his own concert series in Manchester and was musical director for various seasons in the Winter Gardens and Victoria Pier in Blackpool and in both Buxton and Morecambe. (Many readers may remember his daughter-in-law, the renowned organist Florence de Jong, and her equally famous sister, Ena Baga, who has recently had a book published about the family called *Bagatelle— Queen of the Keyboards.*)

The conductors succeeding de Jong —Risegari, Mr Greenwood, Mr G. E. Johnson, Mr Fred Brough, for example—all maintained the reputation of the orchestra. The most famous of all was simply called Toni. 'Everybody knew Toni and everybody knew which pier his orchestra played on.' (Bainbridge, *Pavilions on the Sea*.)

Figure 18: The Indian Pavilion. From Album of Blackpool Views *published by Wm. Z.*

Figure 17: Interior of Indian Pavilion, from The North Pier 1863 to 1913.

Opened in 1877, in the fashionable oriental style, the pavilion was based on the Temple of Binderabund. Seating 1,200, it had excellent acoustics and cost £30,000 including the cost of widening the deck and the bandstand. It was burned out in 1921, rebuilt and, sadly, destroyed again by fire in 1938 when the present theatre replaced it.

Figure 19: The North Pier, 1907.
In this fine 1907 programme, Prof. Speelman conducted works by Rossini, Gounod, Brahms, Edward German and Sullivan, in morning and evening concerts. Mrs Henry Wood sang at the weekend Grand Special Concerts. In other seasons illustrious soloists included Sir Charles and Lady Hallé and Lilly Langtry.

Figure 20: Toni.
Conductor of the eighteen-piece orchestra on the North Pier from 1933 to 1958, Toni was also founder of the BBC Northern Light Orchestra in 1948, doing five broadcasts a week from Manchester during the winter. He resigned from the North Pier at the end of the 1958 season because of plans to reduce the orchestra. It was the end of an era.
'One needs a sedative in this world and a light orchestra playing good music is a wonderful sedative,' he said.
He died in 1972 in his native Hastings.

FOR ALL WHIT WEEK

THE VICTORIA
GRAND ORCHESTRA
40 PERFORMERS.

Conductor - - - Mr. J. W. COLLINSON

Instantaneous success of
THE ONLY PERFECT ORCHESTRA IN TOWN.

FREE OPEN-AIR ORCHESTRAL CONCERT
At 10-30 DAILY.

SPECIAL EVENING PAVILION CONCERT
At 7-30.

VOCALISTS :

Madame MADGE MORGANS, Soprano,
Miss ELLEN SCHOFIELD, Contralto.
Mr. CUTHBERT BLACOW, Tenor,
Mr. ARTHUR WEBER, Bass.

Admission 1s. and 6d., including Pier Toll.

ON SUNDAY—

TWO SACRED CONCERTS

At 3-15 and 8-0 p.m.
THE VICTORIA GRAND ORCHESTRA
And the above-mentioned Quartette of Vocalists.

Special Engagement for Whit Week of England's
Greatest Humorist.

Mr. LESLIE HARRIS

Every Afternoon from Whit Monday till Saturday
Night—The Cleverest, Smartest, and Funniest
Variety Show in Town.

Engagement of the Proligous Lion Comique—

TEDDY WHITTLE

Lancashire's Favourite and Idolised Humorist.
ALSO

THE SISTERS WELBY COOKE, Wire Walkers
Professor KELMAR, Ventriloquists,
ORVILLE PITCHER, The Stump Orator,
Professor WINCKLEY, Bird Warbler.

Solo Pianist and Accompanist—Miss Pauline Stuart.
Admission : 6d. and 1s., including Pier Toll.

FREE OPEN-AIR PERFORMANCE NIGHTLY
At 8-0 p.m. Pier Toll, 2d.

Figure 21 (above): Gazette & News, 1895.
Figure 22 (right): 1932 South Pier programme.
(Courtesy of Blackpool Central Library.)
Edward Dunne conducted a fourteen-piece orchestra, and the
Ladies' Conducting Competition on 22 July attracted thirteen
entrants. Jan Hurst was conductor from 1919 to 1927.
Garadini, George Cathie and Henry Hall
were also popular conductors.

THE ITEMS FOR THE "DAILY HERALD" £5,000 CONTEST WILL BE
ANNOUNCED FROM THE STAGE.

SUNDAY AFTERNOON, AUGUST 14th, at 3-0.

1.—OVERTURE ... "Rosamunde" ... Schubert
2.—TWO MINIATURES (a) "Bird Songs at Eventide" ... Coates
      (b) "A Little Peach" ... Colin
3.—CLARINET SOLO ... "Almora" ... Le Thiere
JOHN BENNISON.
4.—SELECTION on the Works of Liszt ... arr. by Urbach
INTERVAL.
5.—SUITE AFRICANA ... ... Thurban
  (a) "Serenade to Owani." (b) "Moonlight on the Orange River."
    (c) "Prayer and War Dance of the Basutos."
6.—THE SANCTUARY OF THE HEART ... Ketelbey
7.—SELECTION from "Viktoria and Her Hussar" ... Abraham

SUNDAY EVENING, at 7-45.
GUEST CONDUCTOR: ERIC COATES.
The Distinguished English Composer.

1.—CEREMONIAL MARCH ... "The Spirit of Pageantry" ... Fletcher
2.—TWO MINIATURES (a) "The Flight of the Bumble Bee" ... Korsakov
      (b) "A Musical Snuff Box" ... Nickalowsky
3.—A PHANTASY ... "The Three Bears" ... Coates
Goldilocks rises and proceeds to the Bears' cottage. Knocks on the door, and eventually falls asleep in the little Bear's bed. Enter the three Bears. "Who's been sleeping in my bed," says the wee Bear. The chase follows, but the Bears become out of breath, and return home in the best of humour. Goldilocks returns to her Grandma's and relates her adventure. The three Bears decide to nail up a notice on the door bearing the warning: "Beware! Three Hungry Bears live here."
Conducted by the Composer.
4.—OVERTURE TO THE DRAMA ... "Saul" ... Bazzini
5.—SUITE ... "From Meadow to Mayfair" ... Coates
  (a) "In the Country." (b) "A Song by the Way." (c) "Evening in Town."
Conducted by the Composer.
INTERVAL.
6.—THREE WOODLAND DANCES ... Haines
7.—PHANTASY ... "Cinderella" ... Eric Coates
A modern setting dedicated to the "Cinderella" of our imagination. Cinderella is discovered sitting sadly alone by the fire. After a short introduction, the notes of the Flute can be heard faintly suggesting the Fairy Godmother's call "Cinderella." The succeeding agitated movement suggests Cinderella dressing for the Ball, and later drives away in the Fairy Coach. The arrival at the Ball is indicated by the lilt of the Waltz during which the Prince dances with Cinderella. A climax is reached when the clock strikes twelve, our heroine runs, returning to her reflections by the fireside, interrupted again by the Fairy Godmother's call. The Prince's trumpeters are heard in the distance, followed by the State Band leading the Prince's procession in search for Cinderella. The call of the Fairy Godmother brings the Prince to Cinderella's side. Anxious moments follow during the fitting of the lost slipper, but the music surges on to an exultant climax, finishing with a triumphant return of the march theme.
Conducted by the Composer.
8.—SELECTION from "The Quaker Girl" ... Monckton

WEDNESDAY NEXT, SOLOIST— ALGY McCORDALL.
The Wednesday Evening programme is confined to standard Orchestral Works with an Instrumental Soloist, as a variation from the Concerts in which the Popular Song Melodies and Novelty Items are introduced.

7. *Victoria Pier*

BY THE 1890s THE SOUTH SHORE area of Blackpool was growing substantially and plans were made for a third pier. The main promoter was Mr Broadhead who owned the Prince of Wales Baths and theatres in Manchester. There was bitter opposition from the residents, mainly because of the threat of dancing.

Despite the opposition a company was formed in 1890 and building began in 1892. The work was done more rapidly than the other piers because of the Worthington screwpile system, and the Victoria Pier was open in time for Good Friday, 31 March 1893. The Grand Pavilion, however, was not completed until 20 May, when there was a grand opening ceremony. (The name Victoria Pier was changed to South Pier in 1930.)

The pavilion had thirty-six shops and shelters and in the pier's first few seasons these included a bookseller, a draper, a florist, a greengrocer, an ice cream vendor, a photographer, a printer, a wool and fancy haberdasher, and a phonograph stall—a familiar mixture, much the same today.

Like the North Pier, the Victoria Pier had an orchestra of forty players and was even more up-market than the North Pier. Edward de Jong was the first musical director and even organised a winter season, performing *The Messiah* on the pier with his South Shore Select Choir in 1894.

*Figure 23: Letterhead from the 1890s.
(Courtesy of Mr P. Jackson.)*

ENTERTAINMENTS.

VICTORIA PIER
SOUTH SHORE.
Secretary & Manager - GEORGE ROBERTS.

Daily at 10-30, 2-30, and 7-30
PROMENADE CONCERTS by
Herr BLOME'S
FAMOUS ORCHESTRA

At 10-45 and 2-45,
Mr. H. FLOCKTON-FOSTER'S CO.,
"THE IDOLS."
And at 7-30 in the Grand Pavilion.
In Specially Selected Programme.
Stall Seats 6d., Second Seats 6d.
(Including Pier Toll). Wednesday and
Saturday, 1s. 6d.
Special Engagement of TEDDY WHITTLE

GRAND
SUNDAY CONCERTS
At 3-0 and 8-0 by
HERR BLOME'S ORCHESTRA.
Vocalist for Evening:
Miss MARION BEELEY, Contralto.

VICTORIA PIER.

The pretty pier at the south end of the
Borough still continues to draw a full share
of our visitors, and even from "the farth-
est north" of Blackpool. The reason for
this popularity, undoubtedly, is the good
class of entertainments which Mr. George
Roberts and his directors always provide
for their patrons.

Each morning and evening, Herr Blome
and his excellent orchestra play very enjoyable selections; and the programmes are
constantly varied.

Morning and afternoon also, in the open-
air, and every evening in the pretty
Pavilion, Mr. H. Flockton Foster's Costume
Comedy Company, "The Idols," contri-
bute their bright and breezy entertainments,
which are of a character to suit the varied
tastes of large audiences.

The Sunday concerts are always a feature
at the Victoria Pier. The vocalists on Sunday evening were Miss Ethel Holland, contralto; and Mr. Horace Binks, tenor; and
Herr Blome's Orchestra contributed well
selected programmes both afternoon and
evening.

Figure 24 (top left): Gazette & News, *July 1911.*

Figure 25 (left): Gazette & News, *July 1911.*

Figure 26 (above): Victoria Pier, *1901 postcard. 'Providing
"Bright and cosy entertainments" '.*

Figure 27: 1914 Victoria Pier programme.
The Grand Pavilion was completely burned out in 1958 and its replacement, the Rainbow Theatre, was also destroyed by fire in 1964.
A new theatre, the present one, was built within four months, ready for the season's show.

Figure 28 (right): South Pier programme, 1932.
(Courtesy of Blackpool Central Library.)
Seats in the Floral Hall were free except for Sunday evenings
and special concerts, when prices were 4d. and 7d.

Figure 29 (below): Victoria Pier programme, 1914.
(Courtesy of Ted Lightbown.)
Band of the Yorkshire Hussars playing on the pier at Easter.

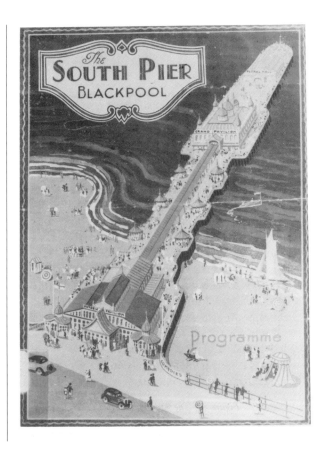

8. The bands played on

BRASS AND MILITARY BANDS were regular attractions on all the three piers. The Victoria Pier, for instance, on its opening weekend featured Besses o' the Barn, the King's Hussars and the Black Dyke Mills bands. Also in September 1893 the Victoria Pier started a series of annual brass band contests (the winners were Black Dyke Mills). The Yorkshire Hussars, Kingston Mills and Lancashire Volunteer Artillery bands were frequent performers, but the main band for many seasons was Herr Blome's Viennese Band.

On the North Pier Bacup, Bury, Colne, Blackpool Excelsior, Raikes Hall and Hulme Temperance bands appeared. For over two decades, right into the 1930s, the Royal Rumanian Band was a great attraction. The band kiosk (now called the Sun Lounge), where Raymond Wallbank is famous for his popular recitals on the Wurlitzer, has been restored in recent years.

Figure 30: The band kiosk, North Pier, c. 1905.
Figure 31: Programme, 1927.
(From Blackpool Central Library.)

The Management of the Central Pier have pleasure in announcing that the following are among the many first class

Bands Engaged for the Season 1927
AT 3-0 AND 7-30.

Sunday, July 10th : DICK, KERR ELECTRIC WORKS BAND.
Sunday, July 17th : NUTGROVE PRIZE BAND.
Sunday, July 24th : IRWELL SPRINGS BAND.
Sunday, July 31st : PENDLETON PUBLIC BAND.
Sunday, August 7th : WINGATES TEMPERANCE BAND.
Sunday, August 14th : BLACKPOOL EXCELSIOR PRIZE BAND.
Sunday, August 21st : DICK, KERR ELECTRIC WORKS BAND.
Sunday, August 28th : IRWELL BANK BAND.
Sunday, September 4th : PERFECTION SOAP WORKS BAND, WARRINGTON.
Sunday, September 11th : DICK, KERR ELECTRIC WORKS BAND.

If the weather is unfavourable these Concerts will take place in the White Pavilion, and an extra charge will be made.

Figure 32: The Rollerator.
(Gazette & News, 13 August 1909.)
Roller-skating was a popular recreation at various periods,
but particularly in Edwardian times, when there were
numerous rinks, costume clubs and skating carnivals in
Blackpool. The Central Pier provided top quality facilities
and was especially innovative in 1909 with the Rollerator,
a mixture of skating and a switchback ride. The skating
was mostly on the centre platform which became the
open-air theatre in 1949, but there was also skating in the
entrance pavilion.

CENTRAL PIER

Secretary and Manager · · · · CYRIL CHANTLER

BIOSCOPE PICTURES
every Morning in the WHITE PAVILION at 10.45.

Fred Allandale's
Daily. 2.45 and 7.30. Pierrots
Acknowledged to be the Premier Troupe in England.

Dancing in the Open Air over the Sea. . .

MILITARY BANDS. :: NUMEROUS SIDE SHOWS.

Swimming and Diving Exhibitions by the most noted Swimmers of the Day.

PIER TOLL, 2d. WEEKLY TICKETS, 1/6.
Special Terms to Large Parties.

Figure 33: Central Pier, from the Official Guide, *1913.*
(Courtesy of Blackpool Tourist Office.)
Joan of Arc was shown by Edison Animated Pictures in 1901
on the Victoria Pier, which earned quite a reputation for
moving pictures with a deluxe cinema opening in 1918. The
1924 tourist guide states, 'The Victoria Pier offers first-class
cinema entertainment'. On the Central Pier animated pictures
were shown on Sunday afternoons and by the 1913 season
they were given every morning in the White Pavilion.

9. *We are amused!*

Figure 34: Electric Grotto Railway. Edwardian postcard.
(Courtesy of Ted Lightbown.)
Blackpool historians think that this ride, or one very similar, was the basis of the 'Fairyland' (on the Golden Mile), sadly burned out in 1914, only to be rebuilt and destroyed again in 1931.

I T IS HARD TO IMAGINE the piers today without amusement arcades, but there were none on the South or the North Piers until the 1960s, when the shore-ends of all three piers were redesigned.

The Central Pier catered more for popular fads such as the Joy Wheel in 1911 and the Auto Skooter, speed boats and cars in the 1920s.

In 1932 there was a weight guessing machine and a guess-your-weight-and-take-your-photo machine (the ticket was 2d. and the photo was delivered in two minutes).

That same season there was also an automatic chip dispenser. A colleague of the author recalls putting a few old pennies in the slot and pulling out from the drawer a greaseproof bag of steaming hot chips together with a metal fork made of two strands of wire twisted together.

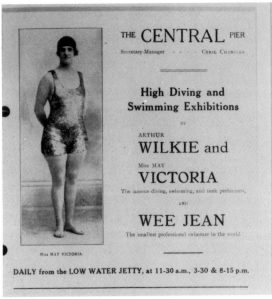

THE **CENTRAL** PIER

Secretary-Manager · · · · CYRIL CHANTLER

High Diving and
Swimming Exhibitions

BY

ARTHUR

WILKIE and

Miss MAY

VICTORIA

The famous diving, swimming, and tank performers,

AND

WEE JEAN

The smallest professional swimmer in the world.

Miss MAY VICTORIA.

DAILY from the LOW WATER JETTY, at 11-30 a.m., 3-30 & 8-15 p.m.

Figure 35: Central Pier programme, 1927.
(Courtesy of Blackpool Central Library.)

'Ornamental Swimming'

Aquatic attractions were introduced in 1871 by the North Pier, which became well known for swimming and diving championships. Professor Johnson was popular for much of the late nineteenth century, and his daughter, Lizzy, swam between the piers in 1878.

On the Central Pier Professor Taylor was featured in 1888 'eating, smoking and writing under water'. Professor Stearne and David Billington, Channel Champion, Graceful Miss Sadie and her troupe of Lady Divers, and Miss Scott, Lady Champion of the World gave displays of 'ornamental swimming'.

Fishing

Another aquatic attraction was, of course, angling. As early as 1899 the piers were noted for their suitability. *Breezy Blackpool*, a guide book for that year, states 'good catches—principally plaice, whiting and codling—are made'. Limited to a hundred members, the South Pier Fishing Club has been in existence for half a century and still enjoys exclusive fishing rights.

An attempt to save the Central Pier jetty from demolition in the 1970s failed, but much more successful was the campaign to save the North Pier jetty. Damaged in severe storms in 1987, it was repaired and reopened in 1991.

Storms were yet another sea attraction—for those watching from the safety of the shore! They were, of course, a great hazard for the piers. Nelson's flagship, the *Foudroyant*, was grounded in 1897, and debris badly damaged the North Pier.

Figure 36: Wreck of the Sirene.
On 9 October 1892 the Sirene *was driven right on to the beach, cutting into the decking near the shore-end of the North Pier, severely damaging the shops and arcade.*
(Courtesy of Ted Lightbown.)

PRICES AND ARRANGEMENTS
FOR SEASON TICKETS

Prices of Season and other Periodical Tickets will be issued to and accepted by Subscribers, subject to the conditions and regulations set forth herein, as under:

	£ s. d.
Single Tickets for Pier and the Company's Grand Orchestral Concerts and Entertainments (Front Seats when available), special occasions excepted, from April 9th to Oct. 4th, 1914, but are not available for Mr. Fred Walmsley's Company, "The Tonics" Entertainments	
To Members of One Household, First Two Tickets	2 2 0
and each Additional Ticket	0 15 0
do., Children over 3 and under 10 years of age	0 10 0
Tickets for Pier only (Special Occasions excepted)	0 10 0
do., Children over 3 and under 10 years of age	0 5 0

All the above-mentioned Tickets are available for admission to the Pier (Special Occasions excepted) until March 1st, 1915.

Monthly Tickets, Pier, and the Company's Grand Orchestral Concerts and Entertainments (Front Seats when available) Special Occasions excepted, but are not available for Mr. Fred Walmsley's Company, "The Tonics," Entertainments	0 7 6
Weekly Tickets, do.	0 3 6
do. (Second Seats)	0 2 6

The above Tickets include Sunday Evening's Concerts.

Weekly Tickets, admitting to Pier only	0 1 6
Single Admission to Pier	0 0 3

Children over 3 and under 10 years of age, half the above prices.

Season Tickets, Mail Carts or Bassinettes and Attendant, Pier only	0 15 0
Monthly Tickets do.	0 5 0
Weekly Tickets, do.	0 1 6
Single Admission do.	0 0 3
Season Tickets, Bath Chair and Attendant, Pier only	1 11 6
Weekly Tickets, do.	0 3 6
Single Admission, do.	0 0 6

*Figure 37 (above): Victoria Pier Programme, 1914.
This fifty-page programme gives excellent details of the entertainments from Easter to October, many advertisements and the season ticket prices (from one guinea to £1 11s. 6d. for bath chair and attendant). Fred Walmsley's concert party, the Victorians, gave three shows a day in the open air and in the Grand Pavilion. His pierrot show, the Tonics, performed in the Entrance Pavilion.*

*Figure 38 (below): Central Pier, 1920.
(Photograph courtesy of Mr C. Critchlow.)
The first pierrot shows were on the beach at, for example, Starr Gate in 1894. By 1899 Sam Hague's Minstrels were on the Victoria Pier in the pavilion. The famous Adeler and Sutton troupe played on the Victoria and Central Piers and many companies such as Fred Walmsley's and Will Catlin's were very popular. The photograph here shows Fred Allendale's Premier Pierrots on the Central Pier. Ernest Binns' Arcadian Follies broadcast on radio many times from the South Pier in the 1920s and '30s. Charlie Parson's Rainbow Pierrots worked on the South Pier from 1952 to 1956, then for eight more seasons on the North Pier.*

10. That's entertainment!

THE BARRINGTON-FOOTE Operatic Company, boxing kangaroo, comic contests, cremation illusionist, harpist, hypnotist, human farmyard, humorist, marionettes, ventriloquist, a vocalist called W. Shakespeare, wire-walker—all these and many others had their place in the early entertainments on the piers.

By the First World War, however, the pierrot shows in their distinctive Pierrot and Columbine costumes, and the more refined concert parties, usually in evening dress and with piano accompaniment, had become major attractions. With competition from mainland theatre, cinema and then television, pier shows adapted to changing taste, becoming the long-running summer season show we know today, with its more sophisticated lighting, choreography, music and costume.

Figure 39 (above right): Blackpool Gazette, 6 July 1946.
(Courtesy of Blackpool Evening Gazette.)

Figure 40 (below right): Holiday Journal, 1931.
Tom Vernon's Royal Follies.

'Uncle Peter'

Peter Webster, born in London, worked as a children's entertainer and his first show was on a raft in Clacton-on-Sea. He came to Blackpool to work in the aircraft industry during the Second World War, after which he presented shows on the South Pier and then Central Pier. Frank Randle, Mike Yarwood, Roy Castle and the Batchelors are just some of the names he helped to stardom. He also personally hosted children's shows and talent competitions on the piers, two a day throughout the season. Millions of holidaymakers knew him as Uncle Peter and there is a pub named after him opposite the Central Pier.

He retired in 1982 to Tenerife, then moved to live with his son in New Zealand, returning to England in late 1992 in ill health. Sadly he died of a stroke in February 1993.

Figure 41: Let's Have Fun.
(Courtesy of First Leisure Corporation plc.)
This title was used for many of Peter Webster's seasons on the Central Pier. His 1955 production was broadcast live on BBC Television, featuring Morecambe and Wise, Ken Dodd, Jimmy Clitheroe and Kenny Baker.

Figure 42 (left): Postcard advertisement. (Courtesy of First Leisure Corporation plc.)

Figure 43 (below): 1953 North Pier programme. (Courtesy of First Leisure Corporation plc.) Scene from the finale of the 1952 show.

On with the Show!

Composer of hit songs such as 'Among my Souvenirs' and 'Carolina Moon', the first publisher in Tin Pan Alley and founder of *The Melody Maker*, Lawrence Wright was truly the Pop of popular music.

He produced *On with the Show!* on the North Pier from 1924 to 1956, one of the longest seaside runs in the country, presenting the top theatre and radio personalities of the day, such as Frank Randle, Albert Modley, Tessie O'Shea, the Tiller Girls, the Beverley Sisters, and Frankie Vaughan.

Figure 44 (below): Showtime, *1964.*
(Courtesy of First Leisure Corporation plc.)
With ten dancers and a twelve-piece orchestra led by Paul
Burnett, the 1964 show starred Mike and Bernie Winters,
Joan Savage and Jimmy Tarbuck. Tickets for the Sunday
shows featuring Manfred Mann, and the Animals, cost 6s.6d.
and 8s. 6d.

Showtime

From treading the boards as an 'eccentric dancer' doing a Charleston double-act all over the continent, Bernard Delfont became an agent and impresario. He presented *Showtime* on the North Pier from 1957 to 1983, featuring a galaxy of stars as varied as Tommy Cooper, the Hollies, Paul Daniels, the Krankies, Lenny Henry and the Black Abbots.

Bernard and his brother, Lew, formed the Grade Organisation, dealing with theatres, cinemas and agencies, which was sold to EMI, owners of the Blackpool Tower, the Opera House and all three piers. Bernard, now Lord Delfont, was head of the company, remaining so when it was sold to THF in 1967. In his seventies he formed his own company, First Leisure, in 1983.

Figure 45 (left): Showtime, *1980.*
(Courtesy of First Leisure Corporation plc.)
The stars in this production were Cannon and Ball, Roger de
Courcey, Jacqui Scott and Lenny Henry.

11. First Leisure for pleasure

FIRST LEISURE PLC, the present owners of the piers, as well as other piers around the country, have initiated many developments on all three Blackpool piers, beginning in 1984 with the new circus-style façade on the South Pier. The Central Pier theatre was altered in 1986 to a new entertainment concept, 'Maggie May's'.

On the North Pier the company has invested £6 million in a new neo-Victorian façade, a conservatory area near the shore, the re-furbished Merrie England bar, the helicopter, the tram and the carousel.

Figure 46: The carousel being assembled.
(Photograph by Jon de Jonge.)
The centre-piece of the Victorian refurbishment, the two-tier carousel, was commissioned from a specialist Italian firm. Opened in June 1991, it is 35 feet in diameter and can take up to seventy passengers. The cost, including refurbishing the Mexico Bar and adding an extra platform to the deck, was over £1 million.

Also in 1991 the North Pier launched a series of helicopter trips 'recalling Blackpool's days of pioneering aviation, when pleasure planes took off from the sands' (*Evening Gazette*, 28 July 1992). The million-pound scheme, however, has had to overcome some problems with anglers and patrons of the Sun Lounge organ recitals. In an attempt to pacify local residents concerned about the noise levels, the helipad was moved 360 feet further down the jetty.

Figure 48: 'People Mover'.
(Photograph by Jon de Jonge.)
Replica of a Blackpool tram, the three carriages can carry over fifty passengers at 50p per ticket. The total cost, including the track, railings and deck reinforcement, was £200,000.

Figure 47: Rising over the sea, 1991.
(Photograph by Lyn de Jonge.)

Redevelopment plans for the Central Pier totalled £4 million for a two-storey arcade, refurbishing the disco, new shelters, the Wheelhouse Bar and, of course, the Big Wheel itself. Built in Holland, it took a month to install on the Central Pier. The Big Wheel is 108 feet high and can take up to 216 passengers. It was opened on Good Friday 1990 at £1 a ride and averaged 15,000 passengers a week in the high season. The pier had to be strengthened, as one can appreciate, bringing the cost to £750,000.

Figure 49: The Big Wheel, Central Pier, 1991. (Photograph by Jon de Jonge.)

Bibliography

If you have been infected with my enthusiasm and would like to know more about piers there is a wealth of information available. Here is a selection of books which have been especially valuable to me.

Adamson, Simon, *Seaside Piers* (Batsford, 1977).

Bainbridge, Cyril, *Pavilions on the Sea: a History of the Seaside Pleasure Pier* (Hale, 1986).

Blackpool Pier Company, *The North Pier, Blackpool 1863–1913* (B.P.C., 1913).

Dainty, Bill, *Stardust and Sand: 50 Years of Blackpool Entertainment* (Author, 1992).

Dobson, Bob and Bretherton, Doreen, *Fresh Air and Fun* (Landy, 1988).

Eyre, Kathleen, *Seven Golden Miles: the Fantastic Story of Blackpool* (Weaver and Youles, 1961).

Fischer, Richard and Walton, J. K., *British Piers* (Thames & Hudson, 1987).

Freethy, Ron, *Wakes Seaside Resorts* (Faust, 1986).

Greenwood, J, *Blackpool Entertains the Troops* (Author, 1986).

Mellor, G. J., *Pom-Poms and Ruffles: the Story of Northern Seaside Entertainment* (Dalesman, 1966).

Mickleburgh, Timothy J., *Guide to British Piers*, 2nd edn. (Piers Information Bureau, 1988).

Palmer, S., *Blackpool Highlights* (Author, 1987).

Parry, K, *Resorts of the Lancashire Coast* (David & Charles, 1983).

Pertwee, B., *Pertwee's Promenades and Pierrots: One Hundred Years of Seaside Entertainment* (Westbridge Books, 1979).

Rothwell, C., *Bright and Breezy Blackpool: a Pictorial Journey through Blackpool's Past* (Printwise, 1991).

Turner, B., and Palmer, S., *The Blackpool Story*, 2nd edn. (Authors, 1981).

Walton, J. K., *The Blackpool Landlady: a Social History* (Manchester U.P., 1978).
——*Wonderlands by the Waves: a History of the Seaside Resorts of Lancashire* (Lancashire County Books, 1992).

Up-to-date information about piers all over the country can be obtained from the National Piers Society, and the Piers Information Bureau. Local libraries will have the current addresses for both of these.